Short *ish* walks
Truro to Looe

Mark Camp

Bossiney Books · Launceston

All the walks in this book were checked prior to publication, at
which time the instructions were correct. However, changes can
occur in the countryside over which neither the author nor
the publisher has any control. Please let us know
if you encounter any serious problems.

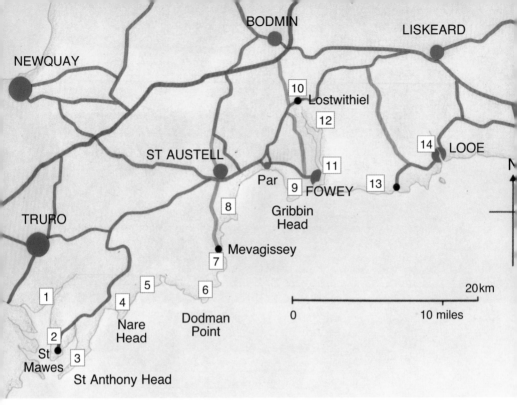

The approximate locations of the walks in this book

First published 2009 by
Bossiney Books Ltd, Langore, Launceston, Cornwall PL15 8LD
www.bossineybooks.com
Copyright © 2009 Mark Camp All rights reserved
ISBN 978-1-906474-08-9

Acknowledgements

The maps are by Graham Hallowell, cover design by Heards Design Partnership.
Boots on the front cover kindly supplied by The Brasher Boot Company.
The photographs on pages 19, 21 and 27 are by the author.
Other photographs are from the publishers' own collection.

Printed in Great Britain by R Booth Ltd, Penryn, Cornwall

Introduction

A 'shortish' walk is intended to take a couple of hours or so, and is typically 6-8 km (4-5 miles) in length. How long you actually take will depend on your fitness, enthusiasm, and the weather conditions. All except one of the walks are circular, and the majority involve either a section of the South-West Coast Path, or a riverside or estuary path, with a rural return.

Safety

Cliff walking can be very exposed; the wind-chill factor is like being out in the Atlantic, and of course Cornish weather can change very rapidly. You need to carry extra layers of clothing, as well as waterproofs, for what is often an abrupt change of temperature between inland and cliff walking. In warm weather, you may well need a hat, and it is sensible to carry a supply of water whatever the weather – dehydration makes you feel tired.

Some of the walks involve fairly strenuous ascents and descents, especially on the coast path. Proper walking boots are vital for grip and ankle support, and a walking pole or stick is useful for balance in the descents. On the inland sections in particular you may well find muddy patches even in dry weather, not to mention briars, thistles and nettles, all of which thrive in our soil, so bare legs are a liability.

The main hazard of walking the cliff path is that for most of the way it is not fenced off from the drop. Go no nearer the edge than you have to: you might be standing on an overhang. Take great care when the path does take you near the edge, and keep a close eye on children and dogs. In many places the cliffs are eroding, so respect diversions.

The maps provided in this book look very attractive but they are only intended as sketch maps, so you may well want to carry an OS 1:25,000 map. OS grid references are given where needed.

The Cornish countryside

Despite many pressures on their livelihoods, Cornish farmers are still trying to make a living from the land you pass through. Please respect their crops; if a few of them haven't yet restored the route of the footpath through their fields, no doubt they'll do so 'd'rec'ly', so go round the edge of the field! Leave gates closed or open as you find them, and keep dogs under control, especially during the lambing season.

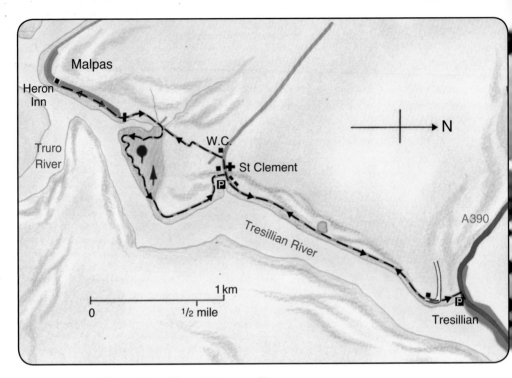

Walk 1   Tresillian River walk

Distance: 7.7km (4³/4 miles) to the Heron Inn at Malpas. Can be shortened to 6km
Time: 2 hours
Character: A predominantly linear walk with a loop at the Malpas end. It starts with a gentle stroll alongside the Tresillian River to the pretty village of St Clement, then crosses fields to Malpas before returning via riverside woods.

Park in a lay-by beside the A390 at the Truro end of Tresillian. A footpath can be found just to the right of the last bungalow on the river side of the road. The raised path leads across a marshy area and is the first of many great places on this walk to spot birdlife.

At the far end of the marsh, turn left along a track and continue around the corner and through a gate. For the next 2km to St Clement the track hugs the riverside. With the tide out, there are vast amounts of mud to gaze at, but with the tide in there are few finer places in Cornwall.

On reaching St Clement take the road up through the village as far as the public toilets. (A short detour to the right leads down to the

4

church, its unusual entrance through an archway below a cottage.) Take the track beside the toilets (PUBLIC FOOTPATH MALPAS) which soon enters a field and climbs to the top. Go through a kissing gate and turn left, then through another kissing gate and turn right. The path descends into a valley.

Once into the woodland at the bottom, the path divides and you have a choice. To cut the walk short, skip the next paragraph.

To visit Malpas, follow PUBLIC FOOTPATH MALPAS over the stream on the right. Ignore the path on the right and continue along the creekside. The path then leads between houses to the road. Continue along the road. The centre of the village is around the Heron Inn, where the Tresillian River meets the Truro River. To return to Tresillian retrace your steps to the wooded valley.

Take the path signed DENAS ROAD. This is a permissive path, quite uneven in places, so care should be taken. It snakes alongside the river through both deciduous and coniferous woodland, with occasional glimpses of the water where gaps occur. When the path reaches St Clement, turn right and return to Tresillian along the riverside path used earlier.

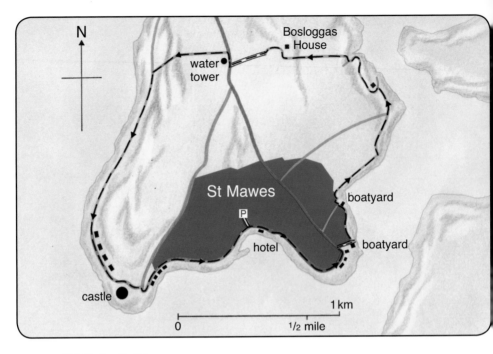

Walk 2 St Mawes

Distance: 6.5km (4 miles)
Time: 2 hours
Character: This walk begins in the yachting haven of St Mawes, then explores wooded creeks and offers fine views of the town and docks of Falmouth, before passing St Mawes Castle. Parts of the walk may become overgrown in summer, and muddy in winter – or even summer! – so it is as well to go prepared for a country walk, with boots and long trousers, rather than for a quayside stroll.

Start from the main car park at the centre of St Mawes. Turn left at the bottom and pass behind the Idle Rocks Hotel. There are some lovely views before the road starts to run between large houses. When it begins to climb, turn sharp right down POLVARTH LANE. At the foot of the slope, by Polvarth boatyard, turn left, PUBLIC FOOTPATH PORTHCUEL CREEK.

This path snakes between gardens to a path junction. Turn right then left on a permissive path behind a large building to reach the river. Turn left. You now leave St Mawes as the path continues along the shore. Entering a field, keep left of the solitary tree in the middle of the field and head for a fingerpost on the edge of a wood.

Once in the wood, ignore the path to the left and proceed downhill towards the river. At a junction, keep left, passing behind a wooden building, and out into another field.

Keep right along the bottom of this field to enter more woodland. The path soon veers to the left then forks right, down to a stile at the head of an inlet. Cross the stile and turn left along the fenced path – beware the barbed wire! Eventually the path arrives at a stile by the entrance to Bosloggas House: turn left here and carry on up the track, which leads to a farm. Follow the track round to the right, through a gate and then on towards the main road.

Turn right, cross carefully, and just after the water tower turn left, PUBLIC BRIDLEWAY CARRICK ROADS. This runs down the right side of a field and can be overgrown at certain times of year. It emerges onto a waterside meadow. Turn left and continue through several more meadows, known as Newton's Cliff, eventually reaching a gate at the end of Castle Drive.

Follow the road in front of the manicured lawns and large houses to reach St Mawes Castle. Turn right at the road junction. From here into St Mawes the road has no pavement. Please be careful, especially in summer when the traffic can be busy. The road runs behind water-front houses before entering the heart of the village amid a vista of thatched cottages and yachts.

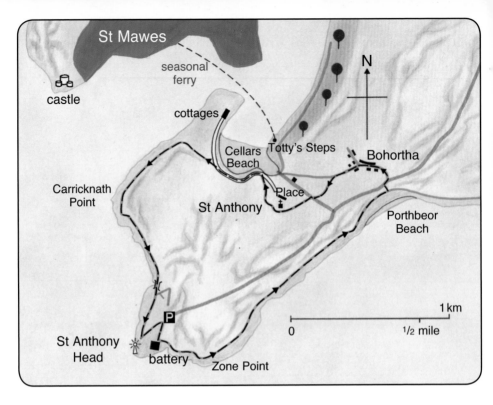

Walk 3 St Anthony Head

Distance: 5.7km (3 1/2 miles) excluding the diversion
Time: 1 1/2 hours
Character: Overlooking the entrance to Falmouth Harbour, St Anthony Head provides some of the finest walking in Cornwall. Not only are there superb views from nearly every point along the walk but there are also Victorian fortifications to explore, and St Anthony lighthouse and St Anthony Church to visit.

Park at the National Trust car park at St Anthony Head (SW 848313) and descend steps to join the South West Coast Path. Turn left and follow the path as it passes the remains of St Anthony Battery, where a viewing table helps explain the 360° vista.

Follow the coast path out onto Zone Point and then for a further 1600m to Porthbeor Beach. This is a popular spot for bathing on warm sunny days. Leave the coast path here and turn left across the field to the lane.

At the lane turn right, then first left to the hamlet of Bohortha. Follow the lane as it swings left between the houses. When it swings

8

right, continue straight ahead along the track (PLACE QUAY) which becomes a path. When the path divides, go over the left hand stile (CHURCH OF ST ANTHONY) and descend to a lane.

Here you may wish to take a pleasant detour totalling 800 m there and back. If so, turn right along the lane, down to the Quay, then take a footpath through a gate on the right which leads to Totty's Steps, where a seasonal ferry crosses to St Mawes.

To continue the route, cross the lane and take the footpath behind Place House towards St Anthony Church. The church is no longer regularly used but is often open. Leaving the church, follow the path as it winds up and round behind Place House, then around the sheltered Cellars Beach. Before you reach the row of cottages, turn left, COAST PATH ST ANTHONY HEAD and climb the hill.

Go through a gate at the top and views of Carrick Roads open up, dominated by St Mawes Castle. The official path drops down to the shoreline and turns left, rounding Carricknath Point.

After just over 1 km you will reach a wooden bridge. Cross and turn right on the coast path (acorn waymark). This will lead you to St Anthony lighthouse which can be visited during the summer months. From the lighthouse return and bear right up the tarmac slope, then climb the steps back to the car park. A detour to the right leads to a bird hide overlooking Zone Point.

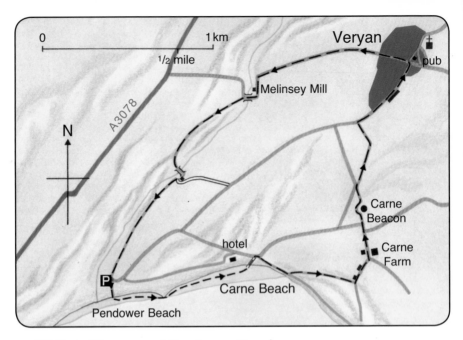

Walk 4   Veryan and Pendower Beach

Distance: 5.8 km (3¹/2 miles)
Time: 2 hours
Character: A wooded valley, a long sandy beach, a Bronze Age barrow,
the longest grave in Cornwall and houses allegedly built to keep the
devil away – all can be seen on this walk on the Roseland peninsula.
Two fairly steep ascents.

Start from Veryan church, just above the gardens and village pond. Walk uphill past the end wall of the New Inn, then after another 30 m turn right, PORTSCATHO ST MAWES. Follow this lane as it leaves the village – it is narrow in places, so take care, especially on a warm summer weekend. The lane descends to Melinsey Mill, where refreshments and craftwork can be bought during the season.

Just after the Mill, the lane climbs and turns sharp right. Turn left here on a PUBLIC FOOTPATH. The path climbs quite steeply, then levels off along the valley side before descending through woodland to cross the stream again at Lower Mill. Please proceed quietly past the houses and up the drive a short distance, before taking the grassy track straight ahead when the drive doubles back on itself.

A gate leads into woodland. Follow the track along the valley bottom to a car park. Continue straight ahead to Pendower Beach. If the

tide is out, it is safe to walk along the beach to the left as far as the slipway at Carne Beach. If in doubt, return to the road and take the coast path, which runs behind the Nare Head Hotel, and joins a lane down to the Carne Beach slipway.

From the slipway, follow the road (COAST PATH PORTLOE) and when it swings inland, turn right through a kissing gate which gives access to fields. Keep the hedge on your right across the first field. Just into the second field, fork left uphill between gorse bushes. Climb steadily to a gate, and then to a path junction. Bear left up a driveway, past a house and onwards up to a lane.

Keep left through Carne Farm. Go straight on at the next junction, then after 50 m continue ahead, PUBLIC FOOTPATH CHURCHTOWN FARM. Keep to the left of Carne Beacon, a Bronze Age barrow said to contain a golden boat. Leaving the beacon, carry on across the field to a stile. Don't join the lane here, but turn right across a second stile.

Keep the hedge on your right across the field. A stile at the far end leads onto a lane. Turn right. At the entrance to the old part of Veryan village you will pass between two round houses: there are two more at the far end of the village, all built just after 1800.

Continue down to the church, where the graveyard contains the longest grave in Cornwall, in which lie 19 of the 24 man crew of the German barque *Hera*, wrecked in 1914.

11

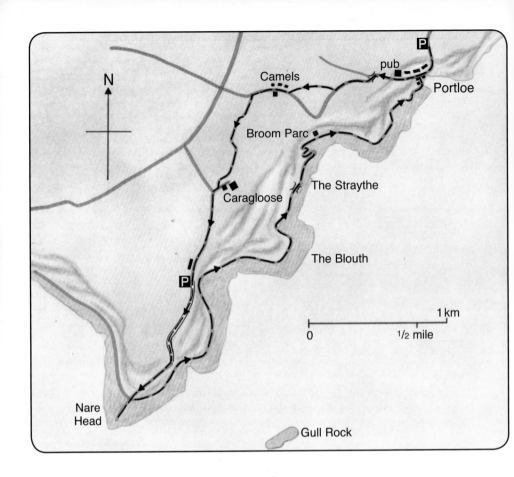

Walk 5   Portloe to Nare Head

Distance: 9.4 km (5³/4 miles)
Time: 2¹/2 hours
*Character: Starting with an inland walk through a tapestry of small
fields, the route climbs to Nare Head before following the stunning
coast path back to the fishing village of Portloe. The village was used
as the setting for the Dawn French TV series* Wild West. *There are
some steep climbs on the coastal section.*

Start in the car park on the north side of Portloe (SW 938396). Follow
the lane down into the village, pass above the little harbour and continue up past the Ship Inn. After crossing a stream, ignore the first
footpath right and continue up the hill. After another 150 m, take the
footpath on the right (unsigned when we last walked it) up steps and
across three fields.

12

Rejoin the road and turn right, to pass Camels Farm. Once clear of the buildings, turn left on PUBLIC FOOTPATH. Cross the stile and keep the hedge on your right across most of two fields, then turn right across another stile (waymarked). Now keep the hedge on your left across further fields to Caragloose Farm. Once beyond the farm, take the gate on the left into a lane. Turn right, then immediately keep left along the lane and it will lead you out to a National Trust car park.

Follow the track from the car park out onto Nare Head where extensive views open up, dominated by Gull Rock about a kilometre out to sea. After visiting the headland, return to the crossing with the coast path, and turn right, following it as it winds, dips and climbs its way back to Portloe.

At one point the path nearly reaches sea level but is soon zig-zagging upward again to the large National Trust owned B&B used several years ago in the TV adaptation of the Mary Wesley novel *The Camomile Lawn*.

From here the path crosses a ridge known as the Jacka before dropping down to the slipway at Portloe. Climb the slipway, then turn right and follow the road above the harbour to the car park.

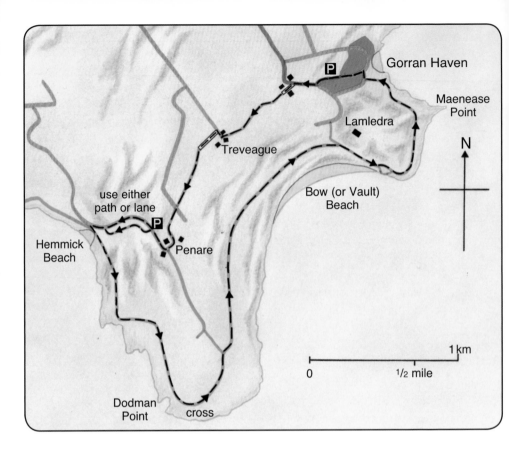

Walk 6 The Dodman

Distance: 8km (5 miles)
Time: 2¹/₂ hours
Character: The Dodman is a major landmark on the Cornish south coast. Make time on this walk from the pretty fishing village of Gorran Haven to visit the secluded beaches at Hemmick or Vault along the way. Some steep climbs and may be muddy.

Start at the main car park in Gorran Haven (SX011416). On leaving the car park turn right and follow the road back up through the village. Ignore the road on the left (Lamledra Hill) and continue to climb gently. When the road bends around to the right, take the PUBLIC FOOTPATH on the left which climbs up a steep-sided valley to Treveague Farm.

Go through the farmyard, turn right then left following signs PUBLIC FOOTPATH PENARE. Take the track across the camping field

14

then along a fenced grassy track to join a road at a T-junction. Go straight across and follow the road down to the small hamlet of Penare. Ignore the two footpaths going off to the left, the second one heading out to the Dodman.

Keep right along the curving lane past Lower Penare Farmhouse and a small car park. Here a footpath can be found on the left which runs adjacent to the lane – useful in the summer when the narrow lane can be busy. Both lane and footpath drop down to Hemmick Beach which, with very restricted parking, is often quiet and is a great place to rest mid-walk.

From the beach retrace your steps to join COAST PATH GORRAN HAVEN VIA THE DODMAN as it climbs out onto Dodman Point. The path passes through the defensive banks of an Iron Age fort before continuing out to the headland where a large cross erected in 1896 stands watching over the channel. On a clear day there is an extensive view both up and down the coast, one of the reasons why a watch house was once sited here, its remains now partly hidden amongst the gorse.

The path now curves away to the left leaving the Dodman and skirting along the top of Bow (or Vault) Beach. This is another stretch of sand worth visiting and can be accessed by a path at the far eastern end, by Cadythew Rock.

Leaving Vault Beach, the path rounds the steeply sided Maenease Point, and clings to the cliff edge as it drops down into Gorran Haven beside its beach. To find the car park, turn left at the foot of Foxhole Lane, up the road that leads off the beach and past the shops.

15

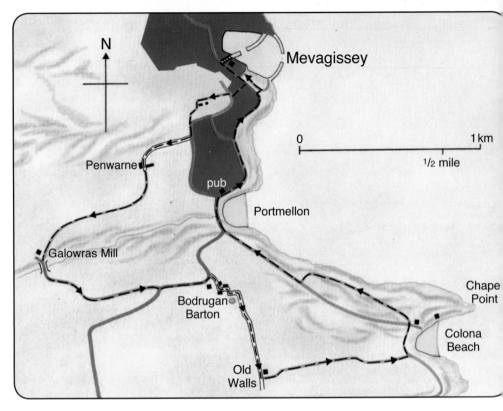

Walk 7   Mevagissey and Chapel Point

Distance: 7.25 km (4¹/₂ miles)
Time: 2 hours
*Character: This walk links the fishing village of Mevagissey with its
smaller neighbour Portmellon. It also gives the walker the chance to
explore a little inland where farming was more important than fishing.
Parts of the path may be muddy in winter.*

Start the walk from Mevagissey Harbour. Head towards the public
toilets on the south side of the harbour where a set of steps leads up
to the road. At the top of the steps turn left and follow the road. Don't
take the path parallel to the road on the left.

   After 200 m turn right up a driveway between Honeycombe House
and Chy-an-Porth. It becomes a path. At a street, turn right and
shortly left, PUBLIC FOOTPATH. After 200 m, on the far side of some
houses, turn left through a field gate.

   Follow the track as it descends, keeping the modern housing on
the left. At a road, continue ahead a short distance before turning

right down a drive to Penwarne, an isolated and reputedly haunted farmhouse. The footpath crosses the yard and carries on behind the farmhouse, before sweeping around to the right and heading up the valley.

On reaching the next house, Galowras Mill, turn left on the lane over the footbridge and follow the quiet lane as it climbs up the valley side to reach the road. Turn left here. At a Z-bend, continue ahead and then turn right into BODRUGAN BARTON.

The footpath snakes through the Barton, now converted into holiday accommodation, and follows a track down to Old Walls. Here take the PUBLIC FOOTPATH which bears left and goes through someone's garden. *Please keep to the path* and leave the garden to enter fields. Follow the footpath down the valley to Colona Beach.

Here turn left along the coast path, passing inland of the houses built on Chapel Point. The path leads to Portmellon and provides great views across Mevagissey Bay.

From Portmellon the route continues to follow the coast path as it joins the road towards Mevagissey. In summer this road can be busy with traffic so you need to take care. At Stuckumb Point, where a green area overlooks the harbour, take the path to the right of the road, which leads back to the start of the walk.

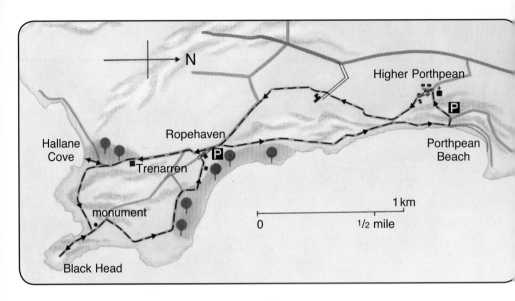

Walk 8 Black Head and Porthpean

Distance: 7.75 km (4³/₄ miles)
Time: 3 hours
Character: Quite a strenuous walk, with half a dozen steep ascents, rewarded with great views over St Austell Bay. The walk is a figure of eight, so it can easily be split into two short walks.

Start at the Ropehaven parking area (SX 033490) just above Trenarren. At the upper end of the parking area a set of steps leads to a stile, signed COAST PATH PUBLIC FOOTPATH PORTHPEAN. The path winds between fields and cliffs, and there are are two steep-sided valleys to cross before you arrive at Porthpean Beach.

Turn left up the beach access road and walk up to the car park. Turn left again and climb the steep hill to Higher Porthpean – beware traffic, because this is a narrow sunken lane.

You will emerge from the lane beside a little church. Take the first left down a tarmac track, past a double garage and through a kissing gate. Keep the hedge on your right all the way up the field. Continue through a broad gap into the next field, and again keep the hedge on your right across the top of the field, parallel to the coast path.

Ignore a sign pointing down to the coast path and continue as far as a set of steps on the right, leading to a kissing gate. Once in the upper field, head diagonally across towards the rooftops of Castle Gotha Farm. Here the footpath crosses a farm track. Turn left and follow the

hedge behind buildings and round to another kissing gate.

Go through this gate and head across the field, slightly to the right, to another gate. On entering the next field continue in the same direction towards the trees on the horizon. The next gate is hidden in the valley. Once through, keep the hedge on your left to join a lane at a gate. Turn left along the lane, back to the parking area.

Walk past your car and take the right fork down to the pretty hamlet of Trenarren. When the lane runs out, keep right on the PUBLIC BRIDLEWAY towards HALLANE. This meets the coast path, but rather than turning left immediately, take a short diversion down to the pretty cove at the bottom. Then retrace your steps and turn right.

The coast path soon climbs steeply and before long Black Head comes into view. When you reach the memorial stone to Cornish historian A L Rowse, you may want to take a further diversion (adding about 600 m) out to the headland for even better views. Then return to the memorial and bear right. Keep right at the next junction, and follow the coast path acorn signs.

You will reach the Ropehaven Cliffs Nature Reserve, where trees begin to obscure the view of the bay. Ignore the next footpath to the left, and continue into the woods. Turn left (acorn sign) beside a bench and climb steeply. The path ultimately emerges on a track. Turn right to return to the parking area.

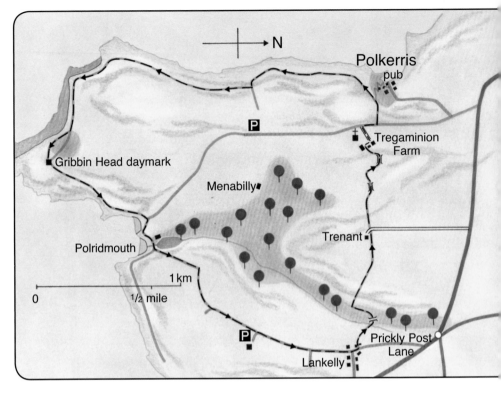

Walk 9   A Menabilly circuit

Distance: 7.6km (4³/₄ miles)
Time: 2¹/₄ hours
*Character: The walk gives you a chance to soak up the atmosphere of
one of Daphne du Maurier's most famous novels,* Rebecca. *The author
lived at Menabilly and it is easy to see where she got her ideas as you
walk around the headland to hidden coves and dark woodland.*

Start from the National Trust car park at Coombe Farm (SX110512)
to the west of Fowey. Walk back along the lane, ignoring turnings, to
Lankelly. Go past the rugby ground and at the next junction keep left
into Prickly Post Lane. Just before the last house there is a track on the
left. Don't take the track itself, but a footpath to the left of it, between
the track and an orchard.

This leads down to a stream and a kissing gate, then under a bridge
which used to carry the driveway into Menabilly. The path, often
muddy, climbs to a stone stile, then follows the hedge to Trenant with
its converted barns. Cross the driveway and another stile, and head

20

up the field with the hedge on your left, before descending steps to a footbridge.

Now keep left as the path follows the contour round a field, before shooting off to the left by a ruined building and crossing another footbridge. The path leads into Tregaminion Farm. Follow the signs through the yard, turning right then left, to meet a lane by Tregaminion chapel.

Turn right along the lane and after 100 m turn left on a footpath. After another 150 m, at a path junction, you could continue ahead then zig-zag down to the little harbour at Polkerris, with its pub and café. It adds about 800 m to the walk (and a climb on the way back!)

Otherwise bear left at the junction on the Coast Path and follow it round to the 19th century daymark on Gribbin Head. From the daymark the path heads downhill towards Polridmouth Cove.

After passing the first part of the beach, keep right at a path junction and continue to the main part of the Cove, with its man-made lake set back from the beach. Cross the stepping stones by the lake and fork left, signed COOMBE FARM. The path climbs the side of the valley, and there are great views back towards the Gribbin. Go through a gate onto a track which in turn leads back to the car park.

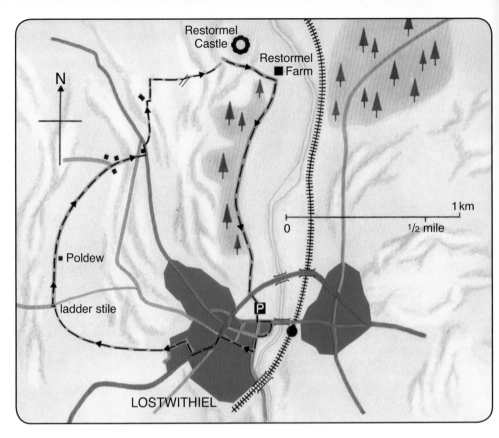

Restormel
Castle

Restormel
■Farm

N

1 km

0   1/2 mile

■ Poldew

ladder stile

P

LOSTWITHIEL

Walk 10 Lostwithiel and Restormel

Distance: 5.75 km (3 1/2 miles)   Time: 2 hours
Character: A walk full of history, starting from Lostwithiel, once the
capital of Cornwall and the chief port on the River Fowey, and passing
Restormel Castle. Field paths and quiet lanes. Some difficult stiles and
one very prolonged climb.

Start from Lostwithiel's main car park, just off the A390 beside the
Community Centre. Leave the car park at the end furthest from the
vehicle entrance, and turn left, RAILWAY STATION. Be careful of traffic
in the town, as there are very few pavements.

Turn right just before the medieval bridge. Follow the road round
to the right then turn left down Quay Street, beside an old building
which was once the Duchy Palace. A little further along, turn right
through an archway which gives access to South Street and continue
all the way up to the main road. Cross (using the traffic lights to your
right) and turn left climbing the hill on the main road to SCRATIONS

22

LANE. Turn right. Follow the lane as it turns left, then when it turns left again, continue ahead, PUBLIC FOOTPATH.

Within a field, keep the hedge on your left, go through the first gate on the left, and keep the hedge on your right up the hill. Divert round some weeds to reach a gate facing you. Once through, still with the hedge on your right, climb to the crest of the hill, go through a metal gate on the right and descend left (north-west) towards two gateways. Take the left gateway and head for the far right corner of the field.

Again there are two gateways. Take the right hand one and turn right. Keep the hedge on your right to reach a wooden stile, which leads to a ladder stile. Cross this, turn left and immediately right along a lane. Follow the lane past Poldew, continue ahead at a lane junction and descend to another junction. Cross the road, and take the track opposite and slightly to your left. Turn left onto a lane and after 20m bear right through a gate. Follow the green track alongside a wood.

After the next stile and gate, keep to the top of the field along a raised track. At the end, cross the stile on the right and turn left, keeping close to the hedge. At the end of the field, cross another stile and keep the hedge on your right downhill. Climb over a metal fence, then the stile ahead of you. Again keep the hedge on your right down to the castle car park.

Now take the lane from the car park, and turn right at Restormel Farm. This lane runs down the valley all the way to Lostwithiel. Cross the main road carefully, and go straight ahead into the car park.

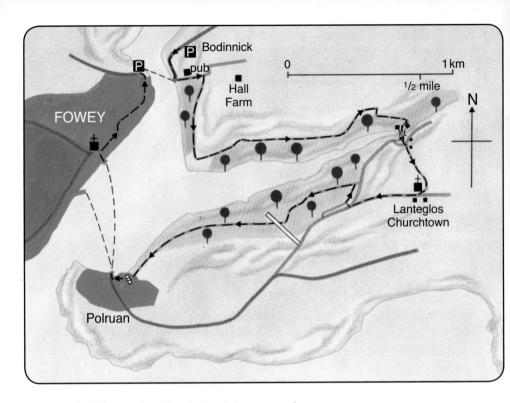

Walk 11 Bodinnick, Polruan and Fowey

Distance: 7km (4½ miles) excluding ferries
Time: 2½ hours, but depending on ferries
*Character: This walk is a classic, not to be missed. Footpaths follow
the contours above a wooded creek with views out to sea, you take
two ferry rides across a busy river, and you have a chance to window
shop in the town of Fowey. In addition, the whole area is soaked in
the ghost of Daphne du Maurier. You will need money for both ferries.
Some steep climbs involved, the paths may be muddy.*

Start from the small Bodinnick car park – on the left hand side as
you drive down towards the ferry. Walk to the foot of the hill. Turn
left, going uphill past the pub and the small church until you reach a
footpath on the right, signposted HALL WALK POLRUAN.

Follow the path along the top of a wooded hillside. There are stunning views down the river and across to Fowey. When you reach the
granite monument to the Cornish author Arthur Quiller-Couch, or
'Q', the path turns left to follow Pont Pill, a typical wooded Cornish
creek. It leaves the woodland briefly before re-entering it by a lovely

stile and taking you down to the creek. Turn right and follow the track down behind the cottages to emerge on the riverside.

Pont Pill was at one time a busy little harbour but over the years has silted up and can now only be reached on high tides. Cross the footbridge and go straight ahead, to the left of the buildings, ignoring the path signed POLRUAN.

The little footpath leads up to a lane. Turn left here and almost immediately right through a gate, FOOTPATH TO CHURCH. Lanteglos church, where Daphne du Maurier was married in 1932, is well worth a visit before going out onto the lane and turning right. Follow the lane to the next junction. Take the path leading into the woods on the other side of the road, and turn right.

Turn left when you reach the main path and follow it, ignoring side turnings, to Polruan. On entering the village down steps, turn right down another flight of steps then turn left behind the boatyard to the quay. It is here that the ferry runs back and forth to Fowey.

Depending on the time of year, you will arrive in Fowey at either Whitehouse or Town Quay. If it is Whitehouse, climb the lane to the Esplanade and turn right, which eventually leads you to Town Quay. From the waterside head right along Fore Street and follow the narrow road to Caffa Mill where the ferry crosses to Bodinnick.

Once again cross the water and return up the hill to the car park.

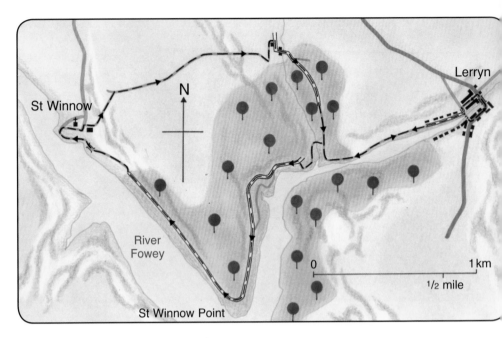

Walk 12   Lerryn and St Winnow

Distance: 8km (5 miles)
Time: 2¹/₂ hours
Character: A delightful and relatively easy walk in woodland beside
the Fowey River leads to the hamlet of St Winnow, with its waterside
church. The return is initially by fields, then a wooded valley.

Start from the car park in the picturesque village of Lerryn. Either
cross the river by the stepping stones or, if the tide is in, follow the
road round to the left and over the medieval bridge. Once over the
river, turn left and follow the lane which leads along the riverbank,
turning into a wide path as it reaches Ethy Woods.

Continue along the path when it bends to the right and heads up a
small creek, then bear left to cross the stream and follow the signed
path and sometimes a forestry track through the woodland. You will
have glimpses of the river on the left until you reach St Winnow Point,
where the Lerryn River meets the Fowey. A cutting has been made in
the woodland, allowing a view downstream towards Golant.

The path now heads around to the right and ultimately emerges
from the woodland into a field by way of a stile. Turn left and cross
two fields before dropping down to the riverbank via a stile and

bridge. Follow the foreshore round – unless the tide is fully in, in which case an emergency route can be found up the bank on the right, shortly after reaching the river – and continue to the old quay at St Winnow.

Turn right at the quay, then right again into the churchyard (PUBLIC FOOTPATH). Go through the churchyard and leave by the main gate. To leave St Winnow, take the footpath which runs behind the cottages on the right. Above this footpath is the farm museum, an interesting collection of countryside paraphernalia.

Follow the footpath as it turns left and heads up an old track. At the top of the slope, cross a stile and head diagonally uphill to the right, as waymarked. Two stiles lead into the next field: turn left and follow the hedge. Cross another stile at the end of the field and turn right, to a gate mid-way along the hedge opposite. Once through this, head diagonally downhill to the far left corner of the field. Cross another double stile, then keep the hedge on your left.

Near the bottom of the field, turn left over a stile and keep the hedge on your right. Pass a cottage then immediately turn right over a stile and down to a track. Turn right.

When the track divides, take the left fork, between two ruined buildings. Follow this track which soon heads down the valley, passing a converted mill-house, until you reach the path junction at the head of the creek. Keep left, and follow the path by which you came, back to the village.

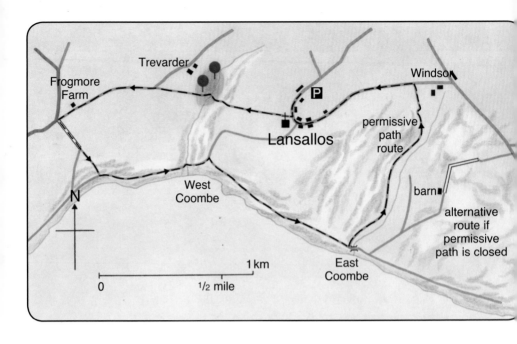

Walk 13 Lansallos

Distance: 7.6km (4³/4 miles)
Time: 2¹/4 hours
Character: Follow in the footsteps of smugglers on this walk which explores the hidden coves between Fowey and Polperro. Several steep ascents and several steep and tricky stiles, with stone steps built out from the side of walls.

Start from the National Trust car park at Lansallos. Turn left from the car park, and walk down the lane to the church. To the right of the churchyard gate, stone steps take you over the wall and along the edge of a field used as a campsite in the summer months. Cross another stile and head straight down the next field, then slightly to the right, to yet another stone stile. The drop on the far side is quite steep – by no means the last you'll meet of its kind!

Cross the small wooden bridge and keep the hedge on your left, down to the bottom corner. Go through the field gate ahead, then through a smaller gate down into the woods, keeping right when the path forks. More stone steps lead down to a bridge over a stream, before the path climbs to leave the woods via a gate.

Cross the field, keeping to the left of the walled trees, and head

28

towards a standing stone. Just beyond this, more steps lead over the wall on the right and drop down into a lane. Turn left and follow the lane for 700m to a road junction.

Just before the junction, turn left through a gate, TO THE COASTPATH, and follow the tunnel-like enclosed path. This was formerly a sand lane, used by local farmers to bring sand and seaweed from the beach to their fields, where it was used as a fertilizer.

Leaving the path, head downhill to the coast path and turn left. The path climbs and dips, passing secluded coves, including Lansallos, where a man-made cutting in the rock gives access to a popular beach. A path leads inland to Lansallos at this point: ignore it and turn right along the cliff path.

After just over 1km, the path descends to a wooden bridge over a stream at East Coombe. Take the permissive path on the left, signed LANSALLOS. Keep close to the stream as you head gently uphill. The valley closes in, and the path snakes left and then right, to ascend some steps into a field. A fenced path leads to a lane.

Turn left along the lane back to the church, then follow the road round to the right and back to the car park.

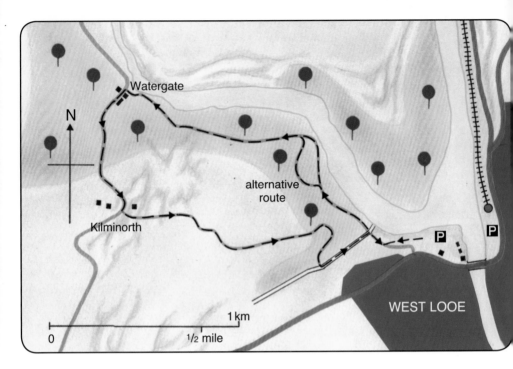

Walk 14   West Looe Valley

Distance: 4.25 km (2³/4 miles)
Time: 1¹/2 hours
Character: Escape into a ancient woodland where a giant once built a wall. With the river never out of view for long and glimpses of the sea towards the end, this is a walk full of the best nature can offer. Mostly on footpaths, with 850 m on a quiet lane. Parts of the path may be muddy. One steep climb.

Start the walk from the Millpool car park in West Looe. Walk away from the town to where a slope leads up into woodland beside the West Looe River. At the top of the slope go through the gate on the right and follow the tarmac track. This will bring you eventually to a flat area of land beside the river. Unless the tide is very high continue on through the gorse bushes and out onto the waterside.

If the tide is high turn left when the tarmac ends and take some steps that wind up and around the flat area. Keep turning right and you will rejoin the path after a slight diversion.

The large flat area is the site of a former boatyard and before that a quarry. It's a nice place to sit and enjoy the river and woodland but

to follow the walk continue to the other side and follow the path as it keeps close to the edge of the wood, running along the foreshore of the river. This is why the other path is recommended if the tide is in.

The path now starts to climb away from the river into the woods, passing the high water alternative route on the left.

By ignoring side turnings you will eventually end up leaving the woods at the little hamlet of Watergate. On reaching the lane, turn left and head uphill.

At Kilminorth, where the lane goes around to the right, take the footpath on the left. This section of the path may be muddy.

The footpath curves around to the right, following an old hedge. At the top of the field, turn left through a gateway and you will see the town ahead of you.

Walk diagonally right across the field to another gateway. Continue ahead towards the town (east, if you have a compass) and head towards the far bottom corner of the field, where a stile is often hidden by undergrowth.

Once in the woods the path carries on downhill and as long as you keep going down you will end up back at the slope that leads to the car park at the Millpool.

Some other Bossiney walks books for Cornwall

Shortish Walks near the Land's End
Shortish Walks in North Cornwall
Shortish Walks – St Ives to Padstow
Shortish Walks – Bodmin Moor
Really short walks – North Cornwall

'Shortish walks' further afield

Shortish Walks on Dartmoor
Shortish Walks in East Devon
Shortish Walks on Exmoor
Shortish Walks – The Levels and South Somerset
Shortish Walks in North Devon
Shortish Walks – The South Devon coast
Shortish Walks – Torbay and Dartmouth

For a full list of our books covering Cornwall, Devon and Somerset, please visit our website: www.bossineybooks.com